WORKELEVATE
Happier Faster Smarter Employees

A playbook by Progressive Infotech

INDIA • SINGAPORE • MALAYSIA

Copyright © Progressive Infotech Pvt Ltd 2022
All Rights Reserved.

ISBN 979-8-88869-329-2

This book has been published with all efforts taken to make the material error-free after the consent of the author. However, the author and the publisher do not assume and hereby disclaim any liability to any party for any loss, damage, or disruption caused by errors or omissions, whether such errors or omissions result from negligence, accident, or any other cause.

While every effort has been made to avoid any mistake or omission, this publication is being sold on the condition and understanding that neither the author nor the publishers or printers would be liable in any manner to any person by reason of any mistake or omission in this publication or for any action taken or omitted to be taken or advice rendered or accepted on the basis of this work. For any defect in printing or binding the publishers will be liable only to replace the defective copy by another copy of this work then available.

Contents

Chapter 1

Caught in the Storm

1.1

Worry lines were visible on her face as she descended the stairs to her office deep inside the cavernous heritage building in the Fort area of Mumbai. So deeply absorbed was Persis in her thoughts that she had forgotten that there was a lift she could have taken down to the ground floor, where her office was, from the Boardroom on the 4th floor.

This special meeting of the Board, to which she was a special permanent invitee, had been called for addressing the equally special situation that was the result of the Covid-19 pandemic that had raged through the world since early 2020 and brought many successful businesses to their knees. Even though it was a virtual meeting, she liked to come into the office occasionally and work from there, as she lived close by. Otherwise, employees were coming into the office only on a need-to basis. For those who could, work from home was the recommended option. She had gone to the Boardroom as two of the directors had also chosen to come in physically for the meeting. Otherwise, she would just have attended the meeting from her office.

She had scarfed through her memory for parallels to the present situation, but had come up short. There had been scandals and scams, no doubt, but nothing that could match the all-pervasiveness of the pandemic. It seemed to be everywhere.

The bank had been founded in the nineties when the Reserve Bank of India (RBI) issued fresh banking licences after many years, and today, it was considered one of the leading lenders in the country. In fact, most of the banks created in that period, alive with opportunity in the aftermath of the economic liberalization, had gone on to scale up significantly. She was one of the first few employees to join, as a move from the foreign bank she had joined after business school, hopeful of new opportunities. And more than twenty years later, she had become the first female CEO of the bank, when her predecessor had retired.

The Board was conscious of the developments, as a responsible Board ought to be, and sought to create a definitive strategy that would enable the bank to overcome the challenges and, going forward, even benefit from the developments. To be more specific, their concern was more around employees and ensuring they were adequately cared for.

"We are aware that WFH is becoming a norm. How this bank must prepare itself to use this as a competitive tool and build agile, anti-fragile, ambidextrous organizations, is the question before this Board," is how one of the members had phrased the challenge.

Another member added, "Our systems, process and procedures must be ubiquitous and enable employees to work from anywhere, anytime. Our support has to be proactive, and responsive. Will our manual systems be able to learn and unlearn quickly and scale and adapt as per the unfolding situation to support our employees? To stay ahead in the post-pandemic business environment, workplace transformation is necessary as employees are working from anywhere and they need support services essentially."

And the responsibility of preparing a blueprint for the strategy had been placed on her shoulders. Persis' record in shaping some of the people-related strategies and focus may have had something to do with the decision. Otherwise, logically, the Head of HR would have been the right person for this job.

Which was OK. Persis was not scared of taking on responsibility. Stepping up was one of the reasons for her rapid rise in the institution. But it was a situation which was without precedent and about which not much was known. Even the vaccination mandates issued by the government seemed to have been issued in a hurry, without the full testing of the vaccines.

The meeting had ended with a parting shot, which was also a welcome development, from the Chairperson, "Also, we are expanding our business to other locations, thus, a NEW digital workplace transformation strategy is a must. We have in-principal approval from the RBI to open our first overseas branches. At this stage, Dubai is the most likely candidate."

"Care for a coffee?" she said instinctively when she saw Peter Diaz, the CIO, before she had reached her office. Like her, Peter also occasionally popped into the office.

Since the pandemic had set in, she had had to work fairly closely with Peter to ensure that the technology backbone of the bank stayed up and running. Peter had taken centre stage during the period and impressed everyone with his meticulous and pragmatic approach to problems. His smuggling in of a few staff members of the IT Managed Services vendor into the Data Centre in Chennai and arranging for their stay and food within the office premises, so that they did not need to risk being caught out during the lockdown, had become a well-known story within the bank. This had been a contributor to the almost seamless functioning of most parts of the bank during the challenging period.

Not one to say no to the CEO without good reason, Peter walked to the coffee machine with Persis and they both walked back to Peter's office, during which time she apprised him of the ask.

"Well, you should be glad you are the CEO of a bank. Thankfully, our products are already virtual. No, I am not talking about virtual money. I am talking about money as we know it today, which is managed virtually. There is no physicality in it. Mostly, it is just accounting entries one needs to pass. When we give a loan, what do we do? We pass an entry which shows some numbers in the borrower's account coming out from an asset account of the bank. That is really it."

She had to agree. The only part which was really physical was the drawing and depositing of cash, which had gradually been reducing. Their own cash counters had been reducing. In fact, while the bank was initially on a branch-opening binge to reach out to newer markets, with digitalization, the last decade had actually seen a reduction in the number of physical branches.

"Now imagine your situation if you were the CEO of an airline or a hotel chain. Would you still be trying to ensure that your staff can work from anywhere and still be fully supported? No, ma'am! You would be worried about matters of the very survival of the business."

Once again, in his matter-of-fact and pragmatic way, Peter had managed to put the situation in a logical perspective. Persis felt better. But the problem persisted.

"But how do we ensure that our employees are supported wherever they are working from? If we were an airline or a hotel, we may not have had to worry about it. But since we are a bank, we have to. And find a way that is reliable for both the organization as well as users, and the employees. I don't think sneaking vendor resources into the office in the dead of night can be a strategy that I can put up to the Board."

They laughed. Turning his laptop towards her, he said, "Look, an IT Managed Services vendor has been pursuing me for several weeks. They claim they have a solution for ensuring support even during lockdowns. Why don't you explore their solution? They are participating in a virtual exhibition happening next week. You don't need to go anywhere. Just register and participate from your office."

"Can you please forward it to me?" Persis said, thanked him and walked out of his office.

1.2

"Don't you know what we do here?" asked Dinesh Kumar, the CIO of Hydramedi, the biggest chain of private hospitals in the country, to Suman Gupta, the CFO, who had joined barely a month back, and was still trying to come to grips with a new industry. The question appeared to be in response to Suman's attempt at a discussion regarding the changes that might need to be brought about in the way the company operated because of the proposed IPO (Initial Public Offering).

"To ensure that we are on the same page," continued Dinesh seeing that there was no response from Suman, "Please understand that while we are a for-profit corporation, what we do here is slightly more important than selling carbonated and coloured soft drinks or sleeker motor cars with a video screen behind each seat," taking a dig at for-profit businesses that he believed did not add any value to the world. "We are Hydramedi. We heal people. We cure them of terminal diseases. We do research and constantly endeavour to find better ways to improve human health. We do work that benefits society."

"I know, I know," Suman said placatingly as Dinesh seemed to pause for a moment to collect his thoughts.

Dinesh looked at Suman and said, "You know? Then, you must also know that ensuring there are no delays in getting systems up and running, and a continuous uptime of our systems, is an absolutely essential requirement. It is non-negotiable. If it does not happen, people will die. It is not a case of a hundred bottles not being filled with a carbonated drink. This is serious business."

As there was no question in that statement, Suman kept looking at Dinesh, as if to say, "So?"

Caught slightly off guard, Dinesh said, "And that is the reason why we want to upgrade our internal systems. No, not our medical software. That is state-of-the-art. But the supporting infrastructure that forms the backbone of our services."

"We have been supported by a technology partner who has done a fairly commendable job in keeping us running, without too much damage. We have their engineers located at each of our key sites, who ensure that any technical issue faced is sorted out asap. They have been flexible and provided us with extra hands when we needed them even though it may not have been in the contract. But the pandemic has shown us that the arrangement is not enough."

"How is that?" asked Suman.

"Because there have been times during the pandemic when we have been stretched. While medical staff have been operating without fail, even at enhanced levels because of the pandemic-related admissions, the technical support staff have found it difficult to keep up. We eventually had to make arrangements to label some of them as hospital staff so that their movement was possible. Besides, we also housed some of them inside hospitals that have the facilities for overnight stay for staff."

"Did that work?" asked Suman.

"Yes and no. But what we need is a technical support strategy that runs independently of body count and location. That is one thing the pandemic has taught us. It needs to be scalable not by the number of engineers on-site but by the capability of the system. We cannot hope to throw people at the next problem that challenges us. Automation has to be the way forward."

"Thanks for sharing this with me. But for automation, aren't you the right person to handle it? How can I be of help? All I can add to the requirement is to ensure that you know the group is going in for an IPO soon. What that means is that the company has decided it is the right time to sell a stake and list the company. What that means is that we will have a lot of funds for growth without a debt burden. Plans are being made for rapid expansion and scaling up of services and locations."

Seeing that Dinesh was looking on uncertainly, she added, "What that means is that I think there is no better time than now for considering automation where possible. If manual scaling is troublesome today, it will be many times more troublesome as we scale up. So, do it now."

Dinesh thought for a bit and said, "I have set up this meeting with our existing vendor who says they have developed an automation framework through which all that we have talked about will be possible. Can you join me for the discussion as some money-related matters might come up?"

"Should be fine, as long as there is no clash. Can you send me the calendar invite please?"

"Sure," said Dinesh. The roles had somewhat reversed by the end of the discussion and he was the one requesting Suman, but he did not notice that.

1.3

"We have put together a plan for continuance of support to clients. To be honest with you, we have opened up access to our frontline staff members from home which, before the pandemic, was unheard of. They can now access the servers from their home or wherever they are. But this is not across the board. It is only for clients who have accepted the risks that are associated with this move. These are mainly companies with large consumer franchises who cannot afford to not be contactable by their customers. Several other clients want us to assume the risk of allowing staff to connect from home. How can we? It is foolish of them to expect this from us. But the result is that we are losing revenue. Many of these were established client relationships." Arun Sharma, the Chief Operating Officer of Vitalsource, one of the largest pure-play BPO companies in the country, was speaking to Anjan Arora, the Chief Financial Officer (CFO) of a pharmaceutical company.

They had known each other since business school, where Anjan was a year senior to Arun. They were meeting on the side-lines of what was probably the first gathering of industry leaders to be arranged ever since meetings and office work were practically shut down since the pandemic struck in March 2020. Like true corporate veterans, who never lost the chance to spend some company money while expressing great difficulty in doing so, they had been the first to confirm, although they had to take flights to reach the location, while most others were local participants.

Anjan was no stranger to these challenges and nodded in agreement. His company had lost more than half its sales force in the period since the pandemic had started. It was not bad from the financial perspective, as they could not do sales on the street, which was their main job. Besides, some of the production facilities had been rented out to the companies producing medicines for management of the Covid-19 affected people. However, now, with the prospects of physical restrictions being gradually relaxed, they were hiring once again to beef up the sales force. And they were running up against a wall.

"People cannot be hired at the same salaries, for love or money," he confided to Arun. "Even the freshers we are trying to hire seem to have upped their salary expectations. I have already, twice in the last two months, approved an increase in the pay out to our hiring vendors for successful hires. But still, the results are dismal. I wonder if the world as we knew it is gone for ever."

"I agree," Arun said. "We have the same hiring issue. What is worse is that people seem to be leaving without even a job in hand. That has never happened, at least in India, in the twenty years I have been working. We are going deeper and deeper to the bottom of the barrel to hire. As we go deeper and hire less competent resources, our training costs rise on the other end. It would have been acceptable for training costs rising if we were saving on the hiring cost and salaries. We are paying more salaries as well as incurring more costs on training people to operate basic jobs. We are struggling to support our people so that they don't find excuses to simply get up and walk out. With restrictions on physical meetings and gatherings still in place, even supporting employees with the smallest of their queries is a challenge."

"I understand," said Anjan. "Imagine what we have to go through. Our sales people have started to gradually move out into their territories, keeping all precautions in mind. Earlier, they used to come back to their base either in the evening or first thing in the morning and offload all their issues and challenges, which either their boss or the HR team attached to the unit would handle. Now, the expectation is that if they have a query regarding a deduction from their salary while they are on the field, they want it addressed right away. They cannot even wait until they come back to the base location in the evening."

"I can imagine," Arun said sympathetically. "We are also facing similar challenges. To make matters worse, the employees who are plugged in and working, are also not able to work to capacity because of gaps in support. In the earlier model, our technical support vendor had engineers co-located on the premises. They would run to the workstation if an employee was impacted and would get him on his way in almost no time. Now, with people working from home, we cannot have that service. It is not possible. But employees, at least the older ones, are stuck in a time warp. They don't understand that they cannot be getting an engineer to visit them. They need to either do some self-resolution or get an engineer to guide them on the phone. Only in extreme cases do they need to either bring the device in or get an engineer to visit. Productivity is down by over 10 per cent. And despite the market situation of hiring, we have had to take disciplinary action against a couple of people who we felt were taking advantage and wilfully not cooperating."

"I wonder what the solution can be," said Anjan. "It certainly cannot go on like this for much longer."

"We are exploring options for employee support, and also, how to keep in constant contact with them. With virtual work, there is now the stress of a different type; of loneliness, of isolation. We need to worry about that," said Arun. Then, as an afterthought, he added, "I am attending a virtual conference next week. I have booked a slot with a service provider who claims they have a solution for this problem. Would you like to join me in the discussion? You can join me in my slot or you can book an independent one for yourself. It's up to you."

"Sure, I can join you. Perhaps, we will be able to gather more based on the questions the other person is asking. It works for me," said Anjan.

"Fine, then," said Arun. "I will send you the logging in details."

The business that they had come to the restroom for having been conducted, they made their way back to the conference room to participate in the ongoing meeting.

1.4

"Look, I understand that business comes first, but it is well known that a chain is only as strong as its weakest link. If we don't shore up our support systems, it is bound to impact business at one time or another." The CHRO of the FMCG major had sought out the CIO and had let off the first volley without any perspective building.

They were in the office, which was a relief. Except for people in their factories and godowns, most other people had been confined to working from home ever since the pandemic had struck the world. Only recently, tentative efforts had been made at testing the waters with a few leadership team members coming in, but the looming second wave was threatening to put an end to all such efforts and adventures.

"What exactly do you mean?" said the CIO looking up at the CHRO.

Between them, Rajat Narain, the CHRO, and Venkat Subramanian, the CIO, were a significant part of the executive team of one of the largest FMCG companies in the country, with a presence in healthcare, personal care, oral care, ready-to-eat foodstuff and many others. The company's investments in technology and processes over the last decade had begun to pay dividends and their growth in recent years had been rapid, in both revenues and profits.

Although, as a senior member of the executive team, Rajat had been in the know of the plans and investments, the one thing that had always irked him was the company's indecisiveness about investing in employees. Several of his plans had been deferred on account of this indecisiveness. At other times, he had been told that market-facing investments will take precedence over internal ones like that on employees.

With over thirty thousand employees on its rolls, it was one of the larger private sector employers in the country of large employers, not counting the hundreds of partners and suppliers who also contributed products and services to the company and were responsible for, at least, a part of its success. As CHRO, Rajat's was an unenviable job, though, of course, an extremely prestigious and desired one.

"Managing a workforce of thirty thousand, of which roughly half are blue-collar workers, is not for the faint-hearted. The range of roles and specializations is vast, spread across the length and breadth of the nation, from the biggest urban sprawls to the small towns in Bihar to the jungles of Chattisgarh and the hills of Uttarakhand. Ensuring the well-being of each employee, as well as ensuring that productivity and quality standards were being fulfilled, are important considerations.

With the rapid growth of business, the lag in employee-centric processes is beginning to show now. Even though the company had built a solid set of HR practices the hard way; from scratch, based on real life experiences and what worked best.

However, generations change, people change and what was good enough yesterday ceases to be good enough for today, let alone tomorrow.

As a simple example, for the HR function, the company has continued to rely on the traditional method of management in a large country; which was geographical. Decision-making responsibility rested with local units, with bigger decisions being referred to regional units, and then, the biggest ones going to the national level. This ensured that the smaller issues, which were the most in number, and often repetitive, were handled quickly, with only a few left over to be decided by the seniors. If there were inconsistencies between different local units on the same issue, it was acceptable in many cases, as the primary unit was the local or regional office. And often, people may not even know or care about what was happening elsewhere.

Since those days, the world has changed. With communication across regions becoming easy and inexpensive, all events have become global events, not merely national. An employee being acted against for poor work quality was bound to be known instantly to employees everywhere in the country. This has coincided with specialization in jobs, resulting in the advancement of functional management over regional management. Simple repetitive issues and queries about salary were now answered by centrally placed resources who had oversight over salary-related matters for the entire workforce of the company in the country. Company phone and email networks, in which the company had invested, have served as the backbone of this process.

Operating in the new environment is becoming challenging. Employee expectations have also changed. Employees now expect anytime access for problem-resolution. It is no longer enough to drop an email and wait for a response in 24 hours. HR staffers are not available on the phone after office hours.

Although FAQs were made and circulated, they were part of a static database and refreshed only periodically. Was that good enough? Clearly no. If an HR policy was being updated, employees want to see the updated policy in the form of a document or updated FAQs almost instantly. This cannot be done with a static database. It can only be done if employees access a live database, which shows the latest information.

Today's employees are digital natives and can comfortably navigate digital tools and access self-help options. By forcing them to ask an HR staffer, apart from slowing down the process, we are actually creating the need for an interaction that is not required and might be distasteful to the employee who has a query or request; he might feel embarrassed asking someone for help."

It had been quite a mouthful, but the CIO was following every word.

He finally said, "So, why are you telling me all this? You should be talking to the CEO, shouldn't you? How can I help you?"

"Employees value an organization that proactively addresses their pain areas whether it is about an application not working or why they are unable to send an attachment. We are getting a lot of HR queries and we need a dedicated 24x7 service desk to address these queries. Also, there are Admin-related queries, which need to be taken care of. Can't we have a solution that covers employee support services with a 360° approach? That is what I am here for. I have talked to the CEO. He has said that there could be a possibility of putting some money on employee-centric activities in the next budget and suggested that I work out a solution with your help."

"*Hmmm*. Good idea. You know, IT has been using different vendors in the four regions plus a few smaller locations for IT support. We are trying to consolidate. In fact, I have a meeting with our vendor in Delhi next week. Would you like to join? It will be a video call. What he is offering to IT may have relevance for HR as well. What do you say?"

The CHRO thought for a bit, wondering if he would be out of his depth in a meeting with a technical vendor, but finally, agreed to participate. "Will you please forward the meeting invite to me?"

"Of course, I will," the CIO concluded.

1.5

"We cannot build a rocket with bicycle parts, can we?" He wasn't quite sure where he had heard it, but the phrase had been stuck in his head for many years. "And if we do build it with bicycle parts, it will have the soul and characteristics of a bicycle, even if we call it a rocket," the speaker had gone on to say. He was always reminded of it when faced with a challenge. And he was certainly in the midst of one now.

A start-up is not for the faint-hearted, but that is what he was now a part of. Rohit Sahni, armed with an IIT degree and a few years with a leading software company, had joined hands with two other colleagues and taken the plunge into the start-up world, trying to make the world a better place and trying to create jobs instead of looking for them.

As the Chief Technology Officer (CTO), his was, perhaps, the most critical role in the early stages of the company. If they don't have a product, they have nothing. After all the deliberations and discussions over the business model and plan, the funding-related expectations, the business requirements documentation and the wireframing, they had finally been able to get to the starting point; of starting to build.

He was passionate about his work and was deeply involved in every aspect. The process of creating the development team had been a laborious and arduous one as he wanted to be absolutely certain about their quality and commitment to the cause. Of course, in deference to the times, the team was a distributed one, working mostly from their home in different parts of the country. For a few people who could not operate from home, he had made arrangements with business centres in their vicinity that they could use as an office.

He wanted the best results from them for their venture. On his part, he wanted to remove every reason for them to not give their best. In his brief experience of working for a corporation, he had realized that issues of a personal nature have the capacity to completely derail an individual's motivation if not handled quickly and correctly. He did not want that to happen in his company.

He wanted them to feel a part of the enterprise. He wanted them to be able to communicate directly with the other leaders in the organization. More than anything else, he did not want procedural, operational and personal issues bogging them down and distracting them from work. It was an important consideration because the world was no longer a 9-to-5 world. Apart from working from anywhere, it was also understood that work could be happening in any segment of the 24-hour cycle that humans have divided the day into. And issues and challenges could raise their ugly head in the dead of night when an engineer based in Cuttack produced her best work but was encountering an issue that needed clarification.

He wasn't talking to anybody. These were the thoughts circling around in his mind, crashing against each other, ebbing away, then flowing back with renewed vigour, just as the rising tide comes in, breaks on the shore and then, regroups and returns, stronger and stronger.

He had discussed this with Rajat Jain, the co-founder who was handling the HR portfolio, along with a young HR manager who had been hired, more on the compensation and benefits side, but as an HR generalist too. She was the go-to person for all team members who had any clarification regarding any HR issue. She was also the go-to person for issues when the employee did not know who to go to. In short, in a short period, she had been able to earn the trust and confidence of the team.

As co-founders, Rajat and he both agreed on the need for world-class infrastructure to support their agenda. But between himself and the HR generalist, they could only do so much. They agreed that the solution would need to be based on technology. But Rajat had no clue about it. Finally, it had fallen back on Rohit to look for a suitable solution.

He had let the word out amongst people he knew in the industry as well as his own colleagues. He had received several suggestions and ideas that he had noted. He was now in the process of going through them one last time before deciding on one, or a few, to pursue more deeply.

1.6

"It is getting repetitive,' the CEO started the dialogue, "and it is hurting business." He was on a Zoom call with Sunil Menon, the CHRO.

"The pandemic, we all understand. It was not caused by you. It was not caused by me. The lockdowns, we can understand. The government decided in the best interest of the nation, and we must abide by the stipulated conditions. Even the desire of mostly single youngsters to run away to the safety of family in probably a safer, smaller town, can be understood." The CEO set the perspective for the offensive.

"When I talk to senior leaders in other companies, I can also say that we are not the only ones impacted by reverse migration. It is a global, or at least national, phenomenon." He paused before saying, "But what I am completely unable to understand is our total inability to stay in touch with our employees and support them during these times of stress. We have people resigning and our HR is coming to know only many days later that the person has joined another company two weeks back. This is unacceptable. How do you think we can run the business in this way?"

If he was perfectly honest with himself, the CHRO would have to admit that he, as well as the HR team, had been taken completely by surprise by the developments.

"And the people we are now hiring, for virtual work, are not only less qualified but also cost much more than the people we are losing. We are sliding fast."

Their company was an established player in the space of IT Managed Services. What that meant was that their clients did not have to worry about managing technology issues on a day-to-day basis. Once contracted, their technically qualified resources would be co-located in the client premises and would respond to every technical issue that was faced by any user. While phone contact was preferred for basic issues, most client staff members preferred calling a service engineer to their workstation to get the issue resolved. This model had been working well and they had built up an impressive client list over two decades in the business. It was a time-trusted model and only minor tweaks had happened over the two decades.

Even supporting their employees who were co-located with clients seemed to be working like a well-oiled machine. An HR relationship manager was responsible for the well-being of employees at each site. One HR RM could be covering multiple teams across multiple sites as most teams were under ten people. The RM would also occasionally visit the site to ensure that their engineers had a workplace and working conditions that were in line with what was available to others in that company and acceptable from the overall perspective as well. If not, the RM would take it up with the business leaders for a resolution with the client. Most business relationships were long and clients were usually supportive of requests that did not ask for more money.

Until Covid-19. The pandemic had thrown all established norms and processes in disarray. The days and weeks after the first lockdown had been implemented were stressful for everyone, both at the personal as well as professional levels.

For their company, it had presented a double whammy. Their clients, who had been forced by the lockdown and the subsequent considerations of safety to reduce and even eliminate working from a common office – and were mostly operating from home at reduced levels of productivity – expected their IT Managed Services partner to be up and running and supporting their employees, even though they could be anywhere in a forty-kilometre radius, as was often the case in a big city. This radius would subsequently increase to five hundred kilometres as reverse migration started.

How could IT support be provided? Initially, for some critical requirements, they had braved the lockdowns and induced, with money, some of their engineers to visit client sites to address their issues. Clients had also been willing to pay extra for that support. But one cannot send a resource based in Noida to Siliguri and Jaisalmer and Gorakhpur to support the employee of the client who has reverse-migrated there. Their operations team had been running a phone-based service to the extent it was possible. Some issues could not be addressed over the phone. But that was not an HR issue in any case.

The HR issue was that their company had been witness to the same event, of reverse migration, that was plaguing many other companies, big and small. While at the start of the pandemic they could hope to induce engineers available near a client site to visit, with their own people moving back to their towns and villages, even that support mechanism ceased to be available, or, at least, substantially dwindled.

In the first wave, employees, even as they started moving back home, had remained contactable and were willing to do what was possible in order to stay employed and receive their monthly pay-check. And that is how most client contracts had been supported by the company. There was a degradation in the service level, but clients were mostly reasonable about their expectations as they were facing the same situation. Only in a few cases had contracts been cancelled, and that was more because of the client going under or substantially scaling back, than any service issue.

By the time the second wave came around, it also brought a complete transformation in the attitude of employees. They were no longer willing to stay for the comfort of the month-end pay check. If they had to work from anywhere, they could work for any employer. This realization led many to look for other jobs they thought they were more suited for. In addition, another unusual development that happened during this period was of people leaving jobs without having another one in hand. Either the loneliness of work-from-home took its toll or they finally decided to act on the work-life balance bit they had been told about so many times, but the Indian version of the Great Resignation had been set in motion.

And they became difficult to reach once they had attained this level of what can only be called nirvana, and ceased to look at their job as the only purpose of their life.

And this is where the CHRO and his HR team had been caught out. Assuming that employees will always look at their job as the primary purpose of their life, like it had always been in a hyper-competitive society with a huge supply of human resources, they failed to recognize the uniqueness of the situation and failed to build the additional bridges that may have provided some relief. Even the HR RMs slackened their grip in the belief that there was not much to do to support people who were already in the comfort of their own home, family and village.

Besides, the circumstances were such that there seemed to be more urgent tasks on hand, which allowed little respite to do forward planning for pieces of the jigsaw that seemed to be in place, like manpower and headcount.

Recovery plans were creating other challenges. Salary expectations of employees seem to have suddenly skyrocketed, even as their expenses had reduced on account of relocation back. Hiring at these rates would create a big hole in the HR budget – an unwelcome development during such times when business continuity was itself a risk.

"So, what is the plan?"

The CHRO shook himself out of his reverie. The CEO was asking a direct question.

"Look, the Operations team will work out a plan to support clients. That is not your problem. But I do need the CHRO to take responsibility for ensuring that hiring and attrition are well managed and that employees, wherever they are, are supported as we have always been supporting them. *Comprende?*"

The final word in Spanish was not a good sign. The CEO used it when he felt that the person he was talking to was not able to understand the gravity of the issue. He promised to have a strategy ready to tackle the situation.

Chapter 2

Navigating to Safer Shores

2.1

"Are we waiting for anyone else?" asked Sandeep.

The question was a result of his long years of experience. As a provider to large corporations, his interaction was with CTOs and CIOs. And even in the third decade of the twenty-first century, they were overwhelmingly male. While he did not in any way disrespect female colleagues and clients, in his line of work, he was used to the decision-maker being male. Hence, he was trying to ascertain if there would be someone else, a male colleague of Persis' who would join. Otherwise, Persis had come into the virtual meeting room almost at the stroke of 10, the hour for which she had managed to book a slot after Peter had forwarded the details to her. It was the first slot for the day.

"I am not," Persis had responded matter of factly. Then, as an afterthought, she had added, "Our CIO Peter might join. He, in fact, was the one who put me on to this conference. I had forwarded him the joining details but I'm not sure if he will."

"Ah, Peter Diaz?" responded Sandeep and smiled. "I have been trying to speak to him but without success. Thanks for letting me know. This gives me a perspective. So, shall we begin?"

"Of course."

"Would you like to start with what challenges you are seeking solutions to so that I can tailor the discussion accordingly?"

"Why don't you tell me the capabilities that you are offering first," said Persis, matter of factly once again. She had felt a little annoyed at what she thought was an attempt at being condescending by Sandeep.

Taking the hint, Sandeep said, without further ado, "Fair enough. Allow me to share my screen."

"What we have here, and what we are proposing, is a framework through which we will be driven by the experience that the user in the system will get. And when I say user, it means the last user, regardless of her rank or role. In fact, the system may actually be blind to the user's rank and role." He paused for a moment to look at Persis' face, to figure out if he was going in the right direction.

It seems he was, since Persis was engrossed, and had failed to notice the momentary lull. In fact, she had been quite taken by Sandeep saying that the experience of the user will be central. That was what she was searching for. If they could provide that, it was worth exploring.

"You see," went on Sandeep, "…most of us have been focused on improving service standards and reduction of cost through optimization. In fact, it has become like a commodity. Do you know any service provider that does not meet or exceed service standards agreed with the client?"

It was a rhetorical question and Persis made no move to respond.

"Of course, everyone delivers the 90% or 100% that has been agreed. Without fail. But what is the result? Are employees happy? Are their needs being met? Are they being supported to deliver their best?"

This was not a rhetorical question. He paused for a response. But Persis shrugged and indicated she did not have one.

"Of course not. Vendors are delivering and exceeding service levels, but user dissatisfaction remains exactly where it has always been. Do you know what we call this?"

"What?" Persis responded finally.

"The watermelon effect. You know how watermelon is green on the outside but red inside? The current arrangement is exactly like that. The SLAs are the green exterior, which create a picture of a perfect world. Slice it open and the red dissatisfaction starts flowing out. Taking an example of an inhouse support service, the IT teams are doing a great job of hitting green SLAs, but their internal customers, the end-users, however, do not always agree and see a broken red. There is a gap."

"I see you are discrediting the IT organization once again, Sandeep," said a new voice in the meeting room. It was that of Peter Diaz.

"Oh, hello, Peter," Persis welcomed him. She was glad he was there.

"Oh, hi, Peter," said Sandeep. "I am glad you could join."

"I had to. Instead of having to field questions from our CEO without knowing what had transpired here, I thought it was better I join in and know first-hand what was happening. But please continue. I am sorry I missed the earlier part, but I will try to catch up on that later."

"Sure. So, I had essentially explained the focus of the new framework we are promoting to Persis and how it focuses on the user experience more than the optimization and SLA hitting that has been the focus of the industry so far."

"Peter, if what Sandeep is saying about user experience being the focus is correct, then this could be a good tool to evaluate," Persis added.

"Let me interject here, Persis," said Sandeep. "What we have proposed here is a framework. A product or tool is the delivery mechanism. Or, we can have multiple different tools integrated into the framework so that it delivers what an organization needs."

"*Hmmm*. So, if I buy what you are selling, what will I get? Can you be a bit more specific?"

It was a direct question, very much a Persis speciality. She was able to get to the root of the issue in an instant.

Sandeep was caught off guard but was able to compose himself.

"Before I answer that, let me paint a picture for you guys," Sandeep said in a bid to address both of them, noticing that Peter was not participating. "Covid-19 has fundamentally altered the way we work. And you don't need me to tell you that. You would know it as well as anyone else. Our workforces are distributed, and getting even more so, with the discovery that much of our work can be handled virtually. It was suspected earlier, but now we know it. Our staff members have also realized that they have a life beyond work. What was unthinkable less than two years back, of employees resigning and leaving without having another job in hand, is happening, which is how some of us have experienced the Great Resignation. Besides, what we call work is also happening round the clock, because people are working virtually and, in many cases, are choosing to do so at times convenient to them, where possible."

Both Persis and Peter had been nodding their heads in agreement.

"So, what does that leave an organization with?" asked Sandeep. "We need to provide systems that are available 24x7 because someone, somewhere may want to work in a particular slot. What does that mean? One of the things it means is that we need to create a support system so that when that person is in the zone and working and a problem occurs, he/she has a mechanism through which that issue can be addressed. Otherwise, from the organization's perspective, it will be wasted downtime because the employee was ready and available, but the system was not.

"Let me stop you here, Sandeep." Persis had assessed the situation and was talking. "I think you have correctly captured the organizational challenges that we face. If your product can address these issues, we will be happy to give it a try. What do you think, Peter?"

Peter, who was used to Persis' style of aggressive decision-making said, "There are two people who would need to sign-off on this arrangement: the CIO and the CEO. And I find that both of them are present here. I don't see why we cannot initiate a pilot. Of course, there will be a process of contracting and legal clearances and all that, and agreement of the conditions under which the pilot will be considered successful, but we can certainly give the go-ahead now."

"Thanks, Peter," Persis acknowledged.

Sandeep was looking from Peter to Persis and then, back again. He had not expected such a fantastic start to this virtual event. Getting an order, even though as a pilot – it would probably be non-commercial – from one of the biggest banks in the country was a big deal.

He could only say, "Well, thank you, Persis, and thank you, Peter. I assure you that we will not let you down. You will receive a draft copy of our standard Terms and Conditions in your inboxes today."

2.2

"Have you heard of Roger Bannister? Sir Roger Bannister?"

"Of course, I have. But what does that have anything to do with your framework?"

"I am coming to that. Do you know what his claim to fame is?"

"Of course. Wasn't he the first human to run the metric mile in under 4 minutes?"

"Absolutely right. Do you know what that means?"

"Now, what could that possibly mean? It means he was the first human to run the metric mile in under 4 minutes. As simple as that."

"What that means is that before him, nobody had been able to run the mile in under 4 minutes. It means he broke a record. It means he pushed the limits of human achievement."

"Of course, he did. What is your point?"

"Do you know that in the eighties, Steve Ovett and Sebastian Coe competed fiercely over the distance and ended up with a record that was almost 10 seconds lower than the one created by Bannister? Do you know what the present record is?"

It was a tangential argument, but Sandeep had been forced to adopt that approach during his meeting with

Dinesh and Suman of Hydramedi, asking them about Sir Roger Bannister and the record for the metric mile.

Hydramedi was a long-time client, albeit a difficult one. They liked to settle any debate or discussion with the argument that they were delivering a huge service to mankind and hence, partners should bend down or accept lower prices or deliver more than committed, or some argument on these lines. Although they did not make money from servicing them, Hydramedi was a highly referenceable account and earned brownie points for them. It had helped them successfully bid for other clients as well. They were also willing to speak to prospective clients and put in a good word for Workelevate, their company.

When Sandeep had explained Workelevate to Dinesh and Suman and highlighted its advantages, Dinesh had sounded skeptical. "But what is the big deal in a framework? Why can a product not do it just as well?" he had argued. "We already have an ITSM ticket-generation tool that helps you and us track resolutions and service levels. If you have the capability of Chatbots and Self-service, why don't you embed it within the ITSM tool so that it stays in one place?"

This was the point at which Sandeep had to segue into the discussion around the metric mile record and how it had improved over time, to highlight to Dinesh that we all need to change and move on. If a tool has been working well, it is great. However, in order to stay relevant, it had to move with the times and adapt its functioning and role so that it can succeed in a changing world. And that is the role the proposed tool would play. It would remove their dependence on the ITSM tool and take it to a playing field situated at a higher level from where they could handle many different moving parts, including the ITSM tool itself. And it did seem to make an impression on Dinesh.

Finally, they had reached the point in the discussion for which Dinesh had requested Suman to join. "So, how much is this going to cost us?" Dinesh had asked. It was a question he was not used to asking. He was used to browbeating the partner by invoking the 'service to humanity' line. But with Covid-19 still a looming threat, and the promise of money coming in through the IPO, had forced him to bite the bullet and ask the question.

"Nothing," said Sandeep.

Dinesh put a hand on his right ear, moved it closer to the screen, and said, "Sorry, can you please repeat that? I could not understand."

"Nothing," repeated Sandeep.

Noticing that Dinesh was a little lost, Suman stepped in and asked, "What do you mean nothing?"

"OK, let me clarify," responded Sandeep.

'So, there is a cost to it; he was lying,' thought Suman.

"The new solution will cost you nothing more than the cost you are paying today in terms of ongoing running costs. You will continue to get the service you are getting, plus the benefit of the additional channels of service such as self-serve and self-heal, at no additional cost per head. The only cost that will come up occasionally is that of integration if there are external tools you are using that need to work with the framework. However, for Hydramedi, at this point, since we are your vendors, we know that there are no such tools, and hence, no additional cost. The other possible scenario is that you buy a tool in future that needs integration. But, I suppose, that is not something we can predict right now, can we?"

"But that is insane. How will you make money?" asked Dinesh, knowing fully well that Hydramedi's vendors rarely made money from them. He also knew that they still wanted their business because it enabled them to make money elsewhere.

"It is simple, really. So far, our support has been based on people. If you add employees, we have to add support staff in a certain ratio. So, on a per-head basis, the cost remains the same. By integrating the automated options for support, we hope to break this linkage. In fact, over time, you could even see the per head cost of support coming down as the model matures."

"Well, will someone explain to me why we are wasting time on this meeting?" Dinesh was back to his usual aggressive self. "We continue to get the same service.

We get the benefit of additional self-serve and self-heal options that we currently don't have. And it does not cost us a penny more. Do you guys think that because we are serving humanity, we are fools to not understand basic math?" he smiled.

Sandeep smiled back. Suman also joined in the smiling.

"Thank you for your support, Dinesh," Sandeep said. "And thank you for joining, Suman. I will be in touch with your team, Dinesh, to work out the implementation schedule. Please share with them the note I had sent to you earlier so that they are aware."

With that, the meeting ended.

2.3

"What Got You Here Won't Get You There." It is as simple as that.

Sandeep had reserved one of his choicest, favourite remarks for a meeting he thought was worthy of it, as he was presenting to not one, but two potential clients at the same time.

The two potential clients were Arun Sharma, the Chief Operating Officer of Vitalsource, one of the largest pure-play BPO companies in the country, and Anjan Arora, the Chief Financial Officer (CFO) of a pharmaceutical company, who had met up at an industry event a few days back and agreed to participate in the virtual event that had been identified by Arun, together, to benefit from the insights each one had.

Sandeep, of course, was quoting the title of the well-known Marshall Goldsmith book, which he was wont to when he was trying to push through some change with a client. It was not just for effect. He truly believed in the relevance of that line. He thought it was the most pertinent piece of *'gyan'* ever for the IT industry. Or any industry for that matter.

Of course, it was after pleasantries had been exchanged and Sandeep had had a chance to thank Arun for bringing Anjan along. "We are not here to sell a product. We are here to introduce a new framework, which we hope will lift the performance of all companies in all industries.

The more the people who get to know about it, the better it will be," he said.

Turning to Arun, he said, "To initiate the discussion, it will be helpful if you can provide me a quick understanding of your business and what brings you here."

Arun thought for a few seconds and said, "We are trying to find ways of keeping our staff engaged." "And satisfied," he added after another gap. He went on to explain to Sandeep the issue of staff having to work from home, which was a new experience for them, as well as the company, and their clients. Since theirs was a Contact Centre operation, most of the time their staff were directly working with the client and their customers. Only when they needed help in the form of technical support or they had a concern regarding HR, would they reach out to someone in the company.

"While in the old model it was simple, they would either walk up to the HR bay and talk to someone, in the post-Covid world, that is not possible. When they call, they are not always able to get through. When HR calls back, they could be busy on a transaction," he explained. "The result? We are seeing them losing their connect with the company. We are seeing them slipping through our fingers like sand. People are resigning without even a job in hand, for the slightest reason, or even without one. That has never, ever, happened. The tools we have tried to use to get them support stay unused. We are struggling."

Sandeep had been listening intently. He already knew the case of Anjan's pharmaceutical company and their struggle to keep up with the sales teams as they started to go back to territory sales. Sandeep was aware that they will attend the meeting together. He could see many similarities between the two and was glad that he could talk together to them. Otherwise, he would have mostly repeated the arguments.

"I understand," said Sandeep. "If it is of any consolation, you are not alone in this. You must be aware that being as widespread as it is, it has also got a name. It is known as The Great Resignation. Fortunately, we believe our solution has emerged out of this situation and should be able to address these issues."

"Can I stop you for a minute?" interrupted Arun. "What exactly do you mean by framework? I saw it has been used in your promotional material quite liberally. I am not quite sure I understand."

"Great question," said Sandeep without thinking, as he had learnt to say whenever a client, or, better still, a potential client, asked a question during a conversation. It was not a reflection on the quality of the poser. "Let me explain," he added.

"What a framework means is that, unlike a product that comes with defined capabilities as well limitations, it provides for all possibilities and situations, without limiting itself to a specific capability set."

"How does that help?" persisted Arun.

"I am coming to that," said Sandeep. "It covers all journeys of the population we are trying to address, in this case, your employees, and tries to create the most optimal solution at each stage. The solution could be offered through a cloud-based technological tool, many of which you might already be using, such as your IT Service Desk, or it could integrate additional technologies that you do not use at present."

Arun's visage displayed his lack of belief.

"So, what happens is that you don't need to trash the existing systems that you have spent time and effort developing. It saves you money. It sits on top of these applications and guides the journeys."

Sandeep could sense a change in Arun's visage.

"And it comes with a service layer. It is not something we deploy and abandon. In effect, you could look at it like this," Sandeep said, switching to a slide in his deck which said: 'End User Support Services' combined with 'Digital Workplace Service Automation' – to provide cloud-first, automated & integrated support to end users.

"End-user support services include Service desk/help desk services, PC provisioning and support services, for physical and virtual devices as well as Mobile device support. You were talking about HR support," he said, looking at Arun's image on his screen, "…were you not?

You know that any self-respecting HRMS or HCM system covers various aspects of HR such as Onboarding and Offboarding, Travel and Expense Management, Leave Management, Benefits/Claim Management and even Employee Communication, does it not?"

With each service mentioned by Sandeep, Arun's eyes became wider and wider. Some of the services mentioned by Sandeep were the ones they had been struggling with. He was struggling to speak.

"But how Workelevate elevates the experience for employees is by enabling them to access the HR system through a user-friendly interface. Not only that, but it also facilitates HR self-service for the most common needs, leaving your HR team to focus on their core work while the querying employee gets the immediate satisfaction of the query."

Perhaps, feeling left out of a conversation he had initiated, Anjan cleared his throat and said, "But what about field services? Is your framework able to handle that?"

"Of course," Sandeep responded without batting an eyelid. "It works in pretty much the same way. Mobile field services offered, as we all know, cover activities like Field Performance Monitoring, Customer Experience, Management and even a Content Repository. In the same manner, as it becomes a user-friendly access and query-resolution pathway for HR queries, Workelevate also elevates the experience of your field services by giving the field staff a window for immediate resolution of many of their queries and issues."

"*Hmmm*," responded Anjan. He could see that there was relevance to what their need was, but he would need to discuss this with others. "Can you send us a proposal of what you are offering for field services?" he asked.

"Of course," said Sandeep. I will send you the same presentation that I have shared with you, along with a proposal for implementation specifically for field services. We can take it from there."

"Perfect," said Anjan.

Sandeep looked at Arun. He was done with the pitch and was looking for ways to bring the discussion to a satisfactory closure. "When can we begin a trial?" said Arun. He was excited by what he had seen. He had the CEO's mandate to implement a suitable solution and hence, did not need other sign-offs, at least for a trial.

Caught off guard, Sandeep made a pretence of looking at his calendar. In reality, he was just buying some time. "How about we meet next week? I will update you on the requirements and the process, and we can get it going from there."

He was glad that he had agreed to this double-meeting. Even though one of the target clients would take time, the primary one was interested, and that was a great result. He expected the secondary client to also be influenced by the decision made by the primary client and convert soon.

"Fine," said Arun. They exchanged numbers and agreed on the schedule and ended the meeting.

2.4

"Thank you, gentlemen, for allowing Workelevate to showcase our advanced capabilities and services that we provide in a world where the pandemic seems to have reset most of the rules we have been playing by." This was Sandeep's expansive way of opening the meeting that had been set up with Venkat, who was an acquaintance for many years since Workelevate had been their managed IT services for the Northern region, which had its headquarters in Delhi.

They had been trying for a long time to get a bigger share of the managed services pie for this marquee client but had not made much progress. With the rules of the game now changing, he was hopeful that they might be able to make progress.

"Thank you, Sandeep," responded Venkat. "First, I must apologize. I have invited my senior colleague, Mr. Rajat Narain, to join me on this call today without informing you in advance. Rajat is our CHRO and is responsible for a large, distributed workforce of many different skill sets. Some people say his is the most challenging role in HR in this country."

"Your colleagues are all welcome, Venkat, and I don't even need to say it. You are embarrassing me by apologizing. I am glad Rajat has joined us for this meeting. It will help me get a better picture of your organization. In fact, if you permit, I would like to request Rajat to share with me what his expectations from this meeting are. I am sure he has some thoughts, and maybe challenges, which is why he is participating in this meeting today."

Before Venkat could respond, Rajat jumped in and said, "Thank you, Sandeep. I will take the liberty of responding though your comment was addressed to Venkat. Yes, Venkat and I discussed this meeting a few days back. Yes, we are facing certain challenges for which we are seeking solutions. Venkat, in fact, suggested I join him today as your solution might be worth considering for our need."

"Thank you, Rajat, for the introduction. Could I request you to please elaborate a little more on the nature of the challenges you are seeking answers for?"

"Why not?" responded Rajat. "You have been working with our company as I understand from Venkat. So, I will skip the basic information like we are the largest FMCG, we have a diversified product range that includes soaps and shampoos, food and oral care, and healthcare and what not, and we have solid processes built up through trial and error over the years."

He paused for effect. Nobody spoke.

"But what was good enough yesterday is no longer good enough today. We have a geographical management structure for HR, which consolidates at the regional level and then, locks into the national structure. This appears to be one of the causes of dissatisfaction is what we believe. Employees today have easy access to employees anywhere in the country, or even the world, for that matter. If a salary issue takes two days to resolve in Mumbai, and one day in Chennai, the guys in Mumbai will be unhappy as they know Chennai folks have better service on that parameter. It could work the other way round for other issues. So, what we want to do is move from a geographical structure to a functional structure for HR. Several other teams are already functional, but HR is not. Can your tool help with this transformation?"

It was a direct question.

"Yes, it can," responded Sandeep directly, following it up with, "…and just for the sake of the record, what we are discussing today is a framework we have piloted for meeting requirements such as yours. It is not a product or platform."

Seeing the quizzical look in Rajat's eyes, he said, and to head off the inevitable question that he had already answered several times, added, "Allow me to explain what I mean. What we mean is that, unlike a ready-to-use platform, which many companies offer and come with defined capabilities as defined limitations, it provides for all possibilities and situations. It does not limit itself to a specific capability set. In fact, instead of cannibalizing on your current tools, our framework builds upon them and integrates them into the overall architecture. It is an architecture that is customised for a client's requirement. Not only that, if a client has two different requirements, there could be two separate architectures that are implemented in your organization."

He made this point because he knew that Venkat and Rajat had different requirements. He did not want to let go of either opportunity. And just as well, because Venkat seemed to sit up when he said this, realizing he was in the game as well.

"How does that help?" persisted Rajat.

"I am coming to that," said Sandeep. "The framework encompasses a hierarchy of solutions that will address a majority of the issues faced by your employees and leave only a small percentage for a higher-level intervention involving real people. Let us take an example," saying which, he shared his screen and brought up the presentation to the screen where solutions were listed.

"The self-service One Click Solutions for Quick Resolutions that constitute Self-service could address Active directory user management, Software provisioning, One-click troubleshooters as well as Printer provisioning while the suite of Self-healing Agent Based Automation for Proactive Remediation could address System Health Monitoring, Bad Block Resolution, Blue Screen of Death (BSoD) Resolution, Preventive Maintenance, Start-up Process Management, O365 Resolution as well as VPN Resolution."

Checking to see their response, and finding a query in their eyes, he added, "That is not all. What is not solved by the self-healing and self-service suites go to the Conversation Chatbot, which, obviously, is available 24x7, as are all self-serve and self-heal options. This chatbot is equipped to provide 24x7 support for IT, HR and other employee support-related queries such as field support. The chatbot is available through omnichannel access from Microsoft Teams, WhatsApp, Slack and web widgets on any browser. Even more interesting is the Chatbot's ability to engage a live agent seamlessly should it feel the need to do so."

He could sense that they were engaged in the presentation. He moved in for the kill. "And then, we begin to reach the human-provided solutions. The Managed End-points suite provides Remote System Troubleshooting and Access, End-point Management, Remote Remediation as well as Patch Management. There is an embedded Ticket Management solution which can integrate seamlessly with your ITSM, HRMS and CRM platforms delivering a Unified Dashboard for End User Experience Status."

There was a hush in the virtual room.

"So, are you saying that wherever an employee is located, she will be able to access this application and get self-service, self-heal and all the other things you have talked about? It does not need to be separate for the Northern region and separate for the Eastern region and so on?"

"That is precisely what I am saying. We are now in a functional world. With due respect, we hardly come across any organisations in our line of work that are structured along geographical lines."

"So, does it mean that you can ensure our employees are supported even while we go through the process of reorganization along functional lines?"

"I will not be able to vouch for the reorganization effort that you plan to undertake. What I can assure you is that your employees will be supported in the manner we tee up the framework as well as the underlying systems."

"Fair enough," Venkat chipped in, indicating that the meeting was over. "We will get back to you soon. In fact, why don't you send us a proposal for the HR support that Rajat spoke about? We can base our internal discussions on that."

Venkat had concluded that since the HR need seemed to be urgent, it might be a good idea to initiate the engagement with HR, and based on the outcome, expand to cover the IT support requirements. He shared this with Rajat separately. Rajat seemed to be in agreement. He could see some positive outcomes for employee support. The battle to get investment dollars for an HR application was still not over though.

2.5

"Plug and play. That is what you need to do. And who can be better placed than you to understand this? After all, the solutions you are creating are designed to do just that. Plug and play. This meeting is almost a sanity-restoring relief for us. Traditional companies have a lot more challenges in understanding and navigating a virtual world. It is not that I am blaming them, but, at times, the debate can be quite sapping."

Through one of the networks that he was a part of, it was either the IIT network, or the IIM network, or the entrepreneurial network, Rohit Sahni had got wind of a few providers that operated in the space where he was looking for support; ensuring that his virtual team was supported every second of the 24-hour cycle and every day of the 7-day week, whenever they needed support. It did not matter what kind of support was needed. It could be an HR query or it could be an issue with a laptop. Today, he was meeting with the representatives of Workelevate, a Noida-based company, which was really a matter of detail as physical locations had become less important in the post-Covid world, especially for businesses like software and banking, whose products were virtual. And it was a physical meeting, as Workelevate had only recently started working from the office two days a week and had checked if he would like to come in for a discussion. He had agreed. From time to time, the desire to engage with other people does get a hold of us, as it had done to Rohit, who had been working almost in physical isolation for several months.

"We are a startup, as you know," Rohit began. "We do not have large teams across which you will be able to spread your investment and cost. At the same time, we don't want to pay a dime more than what a large company might pay."

"That is exactly the point. Most often, costs are higher for a small company for a person-dependent service because there is a certain minimum deployment, below which the service won't work. Until you cross that point, costs will not come down. However, with automation tools embedded and a human support system that is not onsite, that issue gets taken care of."

"Can you tell me what your framework includes?" Rohit asked.

"I was coming to that," said Sandeep and then cued his laptop screen to a slide that said:

'Digital Workplace Service Automation Platform + Digital Workplace Services'.

"You know better than I do that hybrid is the new normal. In fact, companies like yours are getting the advantage of, in a way, leapfrogging across generations. What I mean is that you are setting up shop in a world where hybrid, or substantially virtual, is already accepted. You don't need to go through the pain of discovering the right balance between physical and virtual. You don't need to undergo the issues created by the Great Resignation that we have all heard of. You also don't need to undo any infrastructure you have created for supporting your employees in the previous generation. You are starting with a clean slate."

"Sure. But what about the services?"

"In a world where someone could be working at any point of time, either day or night, from anywhere in the world, Workelevate provides for a 360° support for not only HR but also IT infrastructure. I omitted field support on purpose because you don't have any staff on the field currently. However, if you do add that in future, the same would also be covered."

"And we are not the only ones saying this. This is also the view of analysts of Gartner, the well-known technological research and consulting firm. EUS services include Service desk/help desk services, PC provisioning and support services, for physical and virtual devices and Mobile device support. New digital services include Bring your own device or software (BYOx), End-user support for cloud-based apps, Intelligent automation services, Knowledge management through real-time analytics, Multichannel on-demand support, Peer-to-peer support, Persona-based support, Self-service, Unified communications as a service (UCaaS) and Virtual personal assistants. All of it is covered in the framework."

Rohit was not one to waste time on niceties and pleasantries. "Fine. This should work for us. Can you send me a commercial proposal and indicate the timeframe for starting the service." With this, Rohit got up to go.

"Sure will. Thank you for dropping by. Meeting someone face to face is now rarer, but perhaps, an even more pleasurable event than it was pre-Covid. You will have the proposal within 24 hours."

2.6

"It is not an application. It is a F R A M E W O R K."

Although he had not raised his voice, the spelling out of the word stamped the intent as aggressive.

It had been a busy morning for Sandeep. The participation in the virtual fair had exceeded all expectations. Every slot for virtual visits from interested clients was booked right through the day, many by companies that would be a provider's dream to be called a vendor for. While they were mostly senior professionals who knew what they were talking about, the one point many seemed to miss was that what they were offering was a framework and not an off-the-shelf product that would solve all their problems.

"Nobody wants to make any effort these days," Sandeep moaned to himself.

It had not helped that the current visit was by the HR Head of a competitor, another provider of IT-managed services. Even though the CEO of Workelevate had made it clear that the platform was for everyone, including competitors, when it came down to the frontline sales teams, a competitor was, perhaps, considered to be a lower form of human life than other regular clients, even though that competitor was also a potential client. In some ways, perhaps, an even more important one as it would give them the bragging rights to say that even the competition was using the product.

Sunil Menon, who was on the receiving end of the spelling out of the word, ignored the slight. Only a few days back he had been at the receiving end of a word being called out in Spanish by his CEO. He was in a tight spot and was feeling the heat. He was trying to stay focused on the task at hand so that he could engineer a recovery from their present predicament. He had been searching feverishly for potential answers to the predicament the company, and by extension, himself – since the issue was related to HR – was in. He had already spoken to a couple of vendors for possible solutions. He had also been pointed to Workelevate, which is how he had registered for the virtual fair participation today, even though he knew that it was a competitor. Any solution would do at this time that could help even a little, was his frame of mind.

"Just to be clear," he cleared his throat and said, "Our employees work from anywhere. When I say anywhere, I really mean anywhere. Not only could they be attached to any of our sites across the country, but they could also be working for any of the clients supported by that office who could, again, have workplaces and people anywhere. So, in a way, it is 2x anywhere that I am talking about."

Sandeep had gotten control of himself. He said, "Thank you for clarifying. I may be repeating some parts of this, but our framework is applicable for all Managed Workplace Services, which includes End-User Support Services (EUS) as well as new digital workplace services. What it does is provide cloud-first, automated and integrated support to end users. Whether the degree of anywhere is x or 2x or 5x is immaterial. All degrees of anywhere are supported."

"Thanks. But what are some of the services that you can provide?" asked Sunil.

Sandeep cued the PowerPoint that he had shared with Sunil earlier to the slide where the services were listed.

He explained, "The list is long, as you can see here, and we will send you this deck after this meeting. But, as you can see, it will be able to provide Service desk/help desk services, PC provisioning and support services, for physical and virtual devices, Mobile device support, it supports Bring your own device or software (BYOx), it provides End-user support for cloud-based apps as well as Intelligent automation services and Knowledge management is delivered through real-time analytics. In addition, Multichannel on-demand support, Peer-to-peer support, Persona-based support and Self-service options are also available. It also supports Unified communications as a service (UCaaS) and Virtual personal assistants."

"But, what about HR support services? What you have talked about are the services that are typically offered in an IT-managed services environment. Our operations team understands that and it's not a requirement. Our requirement is HR support for our distributed workforce." Although he did voice this, an idea was forming inside Sunil's head. As a member of the senior team, he was aware of the challenges faced by the business team in delivering, especially during the lockdown period. Theirs was the traditional, manual model of service, with an engineer going up to the workstation of a user facing a problem, and fixing it while the employee idled. He was able to see a possible use-case for the business teams as well, even though his mandate was limited to fixing the HR side. He was aware he was under the scanner, and it would be good if he was able to deliver something more than he had been tasked with. Moreover, it would also help in the cost being shared, rather than having to pay out of an already stretched HR budget, owing to frequent hiring and resignations.

"Thank you for asking," Sandeep responded. "Our robust framework is in a position to handle multiple requirements, HR support being one of the clearly articulated requirements. As we have already discussed, it can support work from anywhere as well as anytime work as most of its capabilities can be accessed 24x7. It will enable you to consolidate your HR Helpdesk under one umbrella support system while offering employees what is referred to as a 360° support. Isn't that what we want in the days of the Great Resignation?"

Sunil was not impressed by Sandeep's effort at HR knowledge. "But what exactly are the HR services will we be able to offer?" he asked.

Sandeep thought for a while and said, "Well, Workelevate neither inhibits nor facilitates the offering of any HR service. You can continue to do Onboarding and Offboarding, Travel and Expense Management, Leave Management, Benefits and Claim Management through your HCM system, as you, perhaps, have always been doing. With Workelevate, you get a tool that enables employees to self-serve and releases time from your HR teams' calendars for more productive work. It can even become an employee communication platform. That is what we start with."

Sunil had seen the slide earlier. He was just trying to reconfirm. From experience, he knew that there could be many a slip between the cup and the lip, but the Workelevate offering seemed like a good starting point. Moreover, he was in a position where he was willing to try anything, such was the pressure on him on account of the spate of resignations and resource challenges in the company. It so happened that this was the first real solution he had come across. If nothing else, even if it was not the best solution, it at least would enable him to buy some time and put the correct fixes in place. '*It should do nicely,*' he thought to himself and resolved to put it up to the CEO for approval.

"What about the commercials?" he asked.

"Rest assured, it will be cheaper than any solution you have been using." It was the usual sales response met with disbelief by an industry veteran. "It will be on a per-user basis, depending on the number and types of services used," he clarified, seeing the look on Sunil's face.

"Can you send me a commercial proposal with the various options as well as timelines," Sunil said, indicating it was time for him to go, and without giving any hints if he would be supporting the proposal or not.

"Sure. You will have a proposal with you before the end of the day tomorrow," responded Sandeep.

Although he had been promising today day-end for proposals so far, seeing the number piling up, he had now started to buy an extra day for his team.

Chapter 3

Future Ready

3.1

"It taught us some important lessons," Arun Sharma of Vitalsource said to Persis, CEO of the big bank based in Fort, Mumbai, "like the need for having quality suppliers."

Seeing the quizzical look in the eyes of Persis, he hastened to add, "During our implementation of Workelevate, for example, we faced certain issues, which is understandable and something we were prepared for. They were all handled by the vendor team. They seemed to know what they were doing. But the one issue that foxed all of us for some time was the inability of the tool to communicate with our ITSM system."

Persis was now interested. She had faced her own set of challenges and, as a result, had learned more about technology and systems during their own implementation. "So, what happened?" was the unasked question in her eyes.

Egged on by the interest, Arun added, "Well, eventually, it was not a big deal. Workelevate has established pre-created interfaces with applications with whom they would need to communicate frequently so that a client does not have to do it all over again. Unfortunately, the ITSM system we were using was not on that list?"

Persis had that quizzical look again. With a tone suggesting that it was not a Workelevate issue, Arun hastened to add, "It was more an issue on our side. We are usually very particular about the tools we buy and from whom they are being bought. It seems that at the time, the ITSM tool decision was taken the company was going through a cash crunch, and opted for a supplier who was not so well established but was willing to offer a much lower price. We were swayed by the price. The supplier has had issues with staying afloat and has just about managed to keep the lights on in their company. I am not surprised that Workelevate does not have an interface already worked out with them as the type of clients they work with are unlikely to be using that product."

"So, what happened? How was it solved?" persisted Persis.

"Well, the solution was quite straightforward as I said," responded Arun. "The bigger challenge was in identifying it. Once identified, the vendor initiated the process of creating an interface for the application which was soon completed. And the rest, as they say, is history."

"What do you mean?" Persis asked, perhaps some questions lingering in her mind.

"What I mean is that we are already seeing results. Agent productivity is on the rise. I don't know if you know our business, but the frontline agent is the critical cog in the wheel. Everyone else's job, in a nutshell, is to manage the frontline resource and make sure he/she can deliver optimally. While there is no perfectly defined level, improvement in productivity and availability is certainly a great starting point," concluded Arun.

"That is wonderful," voiced Persis. "Our experience has been somewhat similar. But I nearly had a heart attack during the implementation phase."

It was time for Arun to raise his eyebrow just a bit in the form of a question.

"You know, in my excitement, while implementation was going on, we had a board meeting with some of the members choosing to come to attend the meeting physically. I guess everyone had been fed up being cooped up at home and were looking for opportunities of meeting people."

"True; that was a stressful time," echoed Arun, looking into the distance.

"In my excitement, I invited the board members, after the meeting was over, to witness the new system being deployed. I think I jumped the gun," confessed Persis. "I should at least have taken the CEO of Workelevate into confidence."

"Why, what happened?" asked Arun, seeing that Persis had stopped speaking.

"You know, I had been involved in the design of the system and we had gone through the pathways through which the chatbot queries would progress. I was really kicked by the smart interactivity the system would provide and keen to show it off to the board members, who had, in fact, initiated the project several months back."

"So, what happened?"

"What happened was that when Saloni, the processor who we had requested join us for the demo, asked the system for an explanation of the reason for deductions from her salary, the response was totally unrelated to the query. And that is when I almost fainted."

"You mean had a heart attack?" Arun gently ribbed her.

"Yes, yes, I forgot…had a heart attack," Persis laughed.

"Then what?"

"Thankfully Peter, our CTO, was on hand to handle the situation. He explained that it was a dummy pathway the system was navigating and that the real pathway was yet to be set up. In fact, he pulled out the design then and there and showed the audience what the fully set-up framework would have said in response."

"So, were they satisfied?"

"Well, I suppose not fully. But Peter saved me from a major embarrassment on that occasion."

"What do you intend to use it for?"

"A whole lot of stuff. The services set up for users of the bank include a self-service menu through which they could get a resolution for issues like Active directory User management, Software provisioning, One-click troubleshooters and Printer provisioning. In addition, self-healing options like System Health Monitoring,

Bad Block Resolution, Blue Screen of Death (BSoD) Resolution, Preventive Maintenance, Start-up Process Management, O365 Resolution and VPN Resolution were made available." Persis rattled off these terms without breaking a sweat, something she would have struggled with before this implementation.

"That is an impressive list," quipped Arun.

"And then there is the chatbot; mostly for HR queries at this stage. What is even more interesting is that users can access the conversation chatbot through multiple channels such as Microsoft Teams, WhatsApp, Slack and web widget on any browser.

3.2

By now, a small crowd had started collecting around them.

They were at the annual award ceremony of the industry association, where Workelevate was being awarded as the 'most innovative company.'

They say peer recognition is the highest form of recognition.

In a nation of a billion plus, it is not difficult to drum up support for any cause. The numbers will always be large whether it is voting for a dancer of 'India's Got Talent' or signing a petition for the release of a seemingly innocent person jailed, even though the signatories may not even know where the petition will eventually go or how it will reach the right authorities.

Against this backdrop, it is strange that corporate endorsements at the peer level are few and far between. Perhaps, it is the nature of corporations operating in a hyper-competitive environment, chary of yielding even an inch of advantage. Most of the awards are based on adjudication by a panel of eminences who, in their collected wisdom, determine the worthies. It is usually not left to the peers to vote and decide.

It is an open secret that there are plenty of awards and prize ceremonies for corporations, many even earning the dubious distinction of being 'bought' prizes, a 'sponsor the event and win the prize' type of arrangement. In this cesspool, the prize for the 'most innovative company' was coveted, as it was based on votes by the peer group.

And this year, this category witnessed much more than the usual level of activity. Not only did many corporations who were their clients vote, even some of their competitors, who had benefited from Workelevate and the innovations it had introduced not too long back, had voted in their favor. Some of them were also using it. Like true leaders, they had not kept anything secret. It was an open framework to be used by anyone who saw value in it. If a competitor found value, so be it. This strategy was guided by the philosophy of a rising tide lifting all boats.

Prateek Garg, the CEO, had been invited to deliver an address showcasing the offering. He had done that, sparking admiration amongst attendees who had not yet been exposed to it. Of course, a large number had, since the association had taken steps to invite all clients of the company who were using Workelevate.

Arun and Persis were busy catching up during the break before the commencement of the presentation of awards.

As often happens during such breaks, everyone wants to be seen to be a part of the most exciting group, but most end up making desultory conversation with a random stranger, trying to look busy and important, while keeping an eye out for a conversation that seemed genuine, interesting and important.

The conversation between Persis and Arun provided that opportunity to several participants.

3.3

"So, did it yield the desired results?" The question was asked by Dinesh of Hydramedi, who was trying to plant himself into the conversation.

Momentarily distracted, Persis looked to see who had asked the question, and recognising Dinesh, smiled at him and said, "Of course it did. Why do you think I am here today? Because we are continuing to use it and expand coverage to other services."

Noticing that the crowd was eager for more, she continued, "The task given to me by the board was to prepare the bank for a world where work from home was the norm and use it as a competitive tool and build an agile, anti-fragile and ambidextrous organization. And we had to do this while ensuring that our systems, process and procedures were ubiquitous and enabled employees to work from anywhere, anytime, supported by a proactive and responsive organisation. And also to ensure that we are able to stay ahead in the post-pandemic business environment."

"So, what is the answer?" Dinesh asked. "Were you able to achieve those goals?"

"What do you think? Of course, we were able to. And more. As you might know, we have got permission to open our first overseas branch. I cannot tell you where it is, but you will know soon. What I do want to add is that Workelevate will be included in the initial set of technology solutions implemented."

"Wow! That is impressive." It was the turn of Rohit Sahni, who was getting to be known as a future unicorn by now, to insert himself into the conversation. He had been trying to reach Rajat for exploring a possible association but had been unable to. He saw an opportunity and grabbed it with both hands. And mouth.

"What has your experience been, Dinesh?" he asked, turning to Rajat.

Although Dinesh did not know Rohit, he responded to the question, "Not very different actually."

"What do you mean?" this time, it was Persis who asked.

"What I mean is that the implementation was pretty smooth. I suppose that with the experience these guys have got working with your companies, they would have known what all can go wrong. So, nothing went wrong as far as the implementation is concerned."

There was an expectant silence as Dinesh completed his sentence. Finally, Rohit broke the silence and asked," So, something did go wrong?"

"Of course, it did," responded Dinesh, relishing being the centre of attention. "But it was not like a train wreck."

"What was it?" Arun chimed in with a question.

"What happened was that our staff members refused to change. Despite the training, communication and hand-holding. And what happened was that Workelevate could not realize the benefit they had envisaged they would as a result of the implementation." Seeing the quizzical look on faces around, he continued, "You see, the platform, of course, was meant for improving our services. But Workelevate also had a vested interest in it; they would be able to reduce the number of staff assigned to support us. So, in a way, it worked for us as they worked doubly hard to ensure adoption."

"I disagree with Dinesh," Persis spoke up. "I think you are being unfair to the supplier. They have never shied away from supporting us, whether it benefited them or not. They make a client's problem their problem."

"Of course, I did not intend to discredit them," said Dinesh, with a sheepish look. "They have been a partner for long and we have full confidence and trust in them. I was just pulling their leg, as I often do when I speak to Sandeep or Prateek.

"So, how did you solve the issue?" This was from Sunil Menon, the CHRO of the competitor of Workelevate.

"The old-fashioned way. I don't think there is any other way," said Dinesh. "We identified a group of people who had a lower level of discomfort. These people would be supported by an onsite engineer. Once these people were able to access the full functionality, they would become ambassadors. In addition, we, the partner and us together, held a few team meetings with the objective of hearing them out and responding to each query with transparency after which, all queries and responses were circulated as FAQs demonstrating that they will not be taking on any additional risk and how it would help them perform better."

"So, did the partner not have this in their change management plan?" persisted Sunil.

"To be quite honest, they did," conceded Dinesh, perhaps wary of another interjection by Persis in support of the supplier. "I think we dropped the ball. Our HR assumed that since we have been successfully working with the partner, they will be able to do their job also."

"I see," said Sunil. "In our case, what happened was…"

The bell sounded, indicating that the break was over and the award ceremony was about to commence. The crowd dispersed to take their seats, leaving Sunil in mid-sentence.

3.4

The award was won by… Workelevate.

It was one of those moments when the company had managed to create success not only for itself, but the entire community of business corporations. It was a moment to savor.

It was a beaming team, led by the founder and CEO Prateek Garg, that went up to collect the award.